ECS Task Execution
Common Troubleshooting Steps

Table of Contents

Chapter 1. Introduction

In this comprehensive Special Report, we delve into the robust yet complex world of ECS Task Execution. Essential for those navigating the multifaceted environment of cloud infrastructure, this report is perfect for anyone seeking to streamline processes, tackle persistent roadblocks, or simply enrich their understanding of ECS Task Execution. Boasting a wealth of knowledge derived from real-world scenarios and backed by a plethora of experienced cloud engineers, this extensively researched report provides common troubleshooting steps that can mitigate downtime and enhance your system's performance. If the thought of modern cloud environment challenges feels overwhelming, let's strip down that complexity together – step by step. This report isn't just about solutions; it's about empowering you to better understand, manage, and optimize your cloud infrastructure.

Chapter 2. Setting the ECS Scene

Understanding the fundamental dynamics of ECS (Amazon Elastic Container Service) is integral to unveiling the full potential of this widely adopted cloud computing service. ECS is a highly scalable, high-performance container orchestration service, which has the power to change the way you develop, deploy, and manage applications.

The first route to enhanced navigation of ECS task execution is a solid grounding in core concepts. So let's begin our exploration by setting the AWS (Amazon Web Services) ECS scene.

AWS ECS provides you the ability to run and maintain a desired number of instances of a task definition simultaneously in an ECS cluster. This could not only simplify the process of managing and deploying containers but also forms the groundwork for task execution mechanics.

2.1. ECS Containers Vs. ECS Tasks

An ECS container is a Linux or Windows-based container that is part of a task, while an ECS task is a logical grouping of one or more containers that are deployed with specified settings. It's essential to understand these two concepts as they form the primary building blocks in ECS.

A closer look at the relationship between containers and tasks reveals the inherent flexibility of ECS. An ECS task may consist of a single container or multiple containers working together, with shared storage volumes if necessary. The containers within a task share networking interfaces and resources, fostering interoperability.

2.2. Understanding ECS Clusters

Another pivotal concept in AWS ECS is the 'Cluster', a logical grouping of ECS tasks and services residing within the same AWS region. ECS clusters can accommodate numerous tasks spread across multiple services.

One of the significant advantages of clusters is resource pooling. All resources within a cluster, such as CPU and memory, are collectively managed. This offers an unprecedented level of control and scalability. If a task requires more resources, it can be allocated the same from the resource pool of the cluster, helping maintain optimal performance.

2.3. ECS Task Definition Parameters

In ECS, a task definition presents a series of parameters required by Docker at runtime. It includes details such as the Docker image to use, the required CPU and memory, the Docker networking mode, as well as numerous other parameters.

Fine-tuning task definition parameters is instrumental in optimizing task execution, aiding in mitigating potential roadblocks, and introducing substantial flexibility to application development processes.

2.4. ECS Task Scheduling

Task scheduling is the process by which ECS decides on which instance a task should be run upon. The AWS ECS scheduler performs this vital function, evaluating resources, capacity, and user-defined task placement strategies.

There are three types of ECS schedulers: the `Fargate` scheduler, the `RunTask` scheduler, and the 'Services' scheduler. Each pertains to different execution styles, with `Fargate` being serverless, `RunTask` allowing manual task execution, and 'Services' ensuring long-running tasks are continually maintained at desired capabilities.

2.5. ECS Tasks Vs. Services

While tasks define what to run, services supervise how and when to run it. An ECS service ensures that the specified number of instances of the task definition are running in the cluster. Plus, they cater to a wide array of operational needs like service discovery, load balancing, and rolling updates.

2.6. Diving Into Service Discovery

ECS's service discovery feature auto-registers tasks to DNS names, paving the way for other applications to access them. Given that tasks might not have fixed IP addresses or predictable lifespans, service discovery assumes prime importance in facilitating seamless interaction between them.

Though understanding the numerous concepts that form the foundation of ECS could feel quite overwhelming, it is these intricacies that lend ECS the power to revolutionize task execution. By consciously building on these foundational aspects, we can vastly optimize the design, deployment, and management of applications within a cloud environment.

In the following chapters, we will delve deeper into real-world application scenarios, troubleshooting common issues, and further enhancing your proficiency in ECS task execution. We're just getting started – there's much more to explore and learn in our cloud journey together!

Chapter 3. Unfolding ECS Task Execution

Elastic Container Service (ECS) is an Amazon Web Service that abstracts away many of the underlying complexities of running and managing containers, allowing users to focus on designing and building their applications. One of the core concepts within ECS is Task Execution, which is the process of preparing and running Docker containers on ECS. This chapter will delve into the depth of ECS Task Execution, addressing its ins and outs, from conceptual understanding to tangible steps of implementation.

In order to minutely analyze ECS Task Execution, we will categorize our examination into three primary sub-divisions as follows:

3.1. Understanding ECS Task Execution

ECS Task Execution mainly involves three core entities: The task definition, the task and the ECS Agent. The task definition is a document that describes how a Docker container should launch. The task takes this task definition, pulls the appropriate Docker images, and then runs the containers. Lastly, the ECS Agent is a component that runs on each instance within a cluster. It is responsible for starting, stopping, and managing tasks.

Here is an example of a very basic task definition:

```
{
  "family": "",
  "taskRoleArn": "",
  "networkMode": "",
  "containerDefinitions": [
```

```json
  {
    "name": "",
    "image": "",
    "cpu": 250,
    "memory": 500,
    "essential": true,
    "portMappings": [
      {
        "containerPort": 80,
        "hostPort": 80
      }
    ],
    "environment": [
      {
        "name": "ENV_VAR_NAME",
        "value": "ENV_VAR_VALUE"
      }
    ]
  }
],
"requiresCompatibilities": ["FARGATE"]
}
```

3.2. The ECS Task Execution Lifecycle

When we talk about task execution, it is important to understand the lifecycle of an ECS task. The lifecycle begins when a task is moved to the PENDING state, initiated either manually or through a service, and proceeds until the task transitions to the STOPPED state. The various steps involved are as follows:

1. PENDING: ECS pulls the needed Docker images onto the host machine.

2. ACTIVATING: The task goes through a brief transition period.

3. RUNNING: Containers within the task are running.

4. DEACTIVATING: Another brief transition period as the task begins to terminate.

5. STOPPED: Containers within the task have stopped running.

This life cycle allows ECS to manage precise control over tasks execution lifecycle, ensuring that tasks are executed as reliably and efficiently as possible, which in turn, accommodates high availability and fault tolerance.

3.3. Implementing Task Execution with the ECS CLI

Once we have an understanding of the life cycle, its implementation follows using the command-line interface (CLI). For example, to create an ECS task definition, run a task and eventually stop it, you would run:

```
$ ecs-cli compose create
$ ecs-cli compose start
$ ecs-cli compose stop
```

The ECS CLI supports Docker Compose, a tool for defining and running multi-container applications. It takes in a Docker Compose file, translates it into an ECS task definition, and helps manage the life cycle of the task.

3.4. Troubleshooting ECS Task Execution

Undeniably, when reaching real-world executions, certain roadblocks might emerge. Here are some common problems and their solutions:

1. Service not starting: This can happen occasionally because of insufficiency in resources, issues in configurations, and more. Keep an eye on the events tab in the ECS console for the service, and look for any issues.

2. Task stopping unexpectedly: ECS agent logs can provide valuable insights. Check the logs for indications of connectivity issues, resource constraints, or failures pulling Docker images.

3. Slow startup times: This problem can often occur due to pulling large Docker images. To mitigate this, consider using an image caching solution, or optimizing your Docker images to reduce their size.

This wraps our inspection into the reality of ECS task execution. Once this understanding is cemented, you are well on your way to handling task execution efficaciously, leading to streamlined operations and optimized cloud infrastructure. Never stop experimenting and troubleshooting - the cloud environment is vast and there is always more to learn. In the realm of ECS Task Execution, your journey towards mastering it has just begun.

Chapter 4. Top Ten Common Problems in ECS Task Execution

In the realm of Amazon's Elastic Container Service (ECS), task execution plays a fundamental role. However, numerous issues can arise during the lifecycle of a task. In this chapter, we will discuss the ten common problems often encountered in ECS Task Execution, including providing practical mitigation steps.

4.1. 1. Insufficient Resources

Perhaps the most common problem in ECS Task Execution is the lack of enough resources. This can occur when there aren't enough CPU or memory resources to run your tasks, resulting in task failures or long pending times.

Mitigation Plans: - Monitor your cluster's resource usage to ensure it has sufficient CPU and memory resources. - Implement auto-scaling groups to manage instances within your clusters.

4.2. 2. Resource Exhaustion

This issue is often interconnected with the first. Resources are finite, and while you may have sufficient resources overall, they can be exhausted over time due to long-running tasks or memory leaks.

Mitigation Plans: - Regularly monitor your resource consumption over time. - Design your tasks to efficiently utilize resources and properly deallocate those used when they're no longer needed.

4.3. 3. Task Scheduling Failures

ECS task scheduling failures can occur due to resource deficits, platform version mismatches, or placement constraints.

Mitigation Plans: - Regularly update your images and ensure they're compatible with your chosen platform version. - Reevaluate your task placement constraints and ensure they're not too restrictive.

4.4. 4. Task Networking Issues

Network configuration issues can negatively impact your ECS tasks – this could result from unusable ports or the assignment of incorrect security groups to the task or its associated instance.

Mitigation Plans: - Regularly check your network configurations to ensure they match the specifications of your tasks. - Assign security groups that allow all necessary inbound and outbound traffic for your tasks.

4.5. 5. Task IAM Role Issues

IAM roles are used to grant permissions to ECS tasks. If these roles are not configured correctly, tasks can fail to execute.

Mitigation Plans: - Ensure that your task IAM roles correctly grant all necessary permissions and access. - Regularly review IAM roles and their associated policies.

4.6. 6. Container Dependency Failures

Failure to manage container dependencies can result in tasks that don't run correctly. Your task may depend on other containers to start first before it can run, an organisational dependency that if overlooked, could spell trouble.

Mitigation plans: - Implement container dependency management to ensure the sequential startup of your task's containers. - Regularly monitor and update container dependencies as needed.

4.7. 7. Troubles with TaskHealthCheck

ECS allows for the inclusion of health checks within the task lifecycle. If these health checks fail, it can cause the task to stop.

Mitigation Plans: - Implement regular checks, ensuring that Task's HealthCheck commands are responding correctly. - Review logs after a failed health check to uncover the root cause.

4.8. 8. Frustrations with Logging and Monitoring

Logging and monitoring systems can fail due to misconfigurations, compromised permissions, storage shortfalls, or unavailability of services.

Mitigation Plans: - Ensure that logging, and monitoring systems are configured correctly with unlimited storage or a log rotation policy. - Implement regular audit trails to ensure consistency in logging.

4.9. 9. Task Start Timeout

Tasks failing to start within the ECS timeout period will be terminated, causing abrupt stoppages.

Mitigation Plans: - Monitor task startup times and optimize any tasks that are close to or exceeding the timeout period. - Increase the start timeout if task initialization requires more time.

4.10. 10. Task Lifecycle Event Issues

Task lifecycle event handlers can fail or timeout, resulting in halted task execution.

Mitigation Plans: - Ensuring that lifecycle event handlers are robust against failures and built to retry upon failure. - Monitor the overall duration of your task lifecycle event handler logic and make sure it stays within the ECS time limit for task stoppage.

In conclusion, while ECS Task Execution can be plagued by a myriad of issues, by following proper mitigation plans it's possible to create a resilient, efficient, and performant system. With so many factors in play, understanding common complex problems is the first line of defense. It is our hope that this chapter equipped you with the knowledge to accurately identify these common problems and respond in a way that optimizes your cloud infrastructure performance.

Chapter 5. Demystifying Troubleshooting Steps

Understanding the world of Amazon Elastic Container Service (ECS) Task Execution can be a multi-layered task. However, every complex problem has a simple structure at its heart. In this chapter, we peel back the layers on common troubles that users may run into when dealing with ECS Task Execution in order to understand its complete process, provide troubleshooting strategies, and optimize your cloud deployment.

5.1. Task Fails to Launch

The first hurdle that many users often face is a task failing to launch. Typical symptoms include tasks stopping with a status of `STOPPED` immediately after starting, and tasks failing the ELB health check.

To troubleshoot this issue, follow these steps:

1. Check if your task is using the latest Amazon ECS-optimized Amazon Linux 2 AMI. Remember, the Amazon ECS-optimized Amazon Linux AMI is reaching the end of its support life cycle and you should ensure a seamless transition to the Amazon ECS-optimized Amazon Linux 2 AMI.

2. Evaluate the Amazon CloudWatch logs for your tasks. CloudWatch logs can help monitor, store, and access your log files from Amazon ECS.

3. In your Dockerfile, add simple health check commands to the `HEALTHCHECK` instruction. This will facilitate the detection of task failure at an earlier stage.

5.2. Task Stops Unexpectedly

At times, tasks might stop without any apparent reason. This can be hard to trace unless you deep-dive into the system state.

To troubleshoot, we recommend the following steps:

1. Check your Amazon ECS service event messages. Service events provide helpful information about task changes, be it unscheduled instances or task placement failures.

2. Ensure that your volumes are correctly configured, and there are no issues with storage permission.

3. If your task fails to pull the Docker image, validate your authentication credentials and check if you have internet access or Docker Hub access enabled.

5.3. High CPU and Memory Utilization

High CPU and memory usage by tasks can lead to a slow environment and degraded performance, hampering productivity.

If you face high CPU and memory utilization, consider taking the following troubleshooting steps:

1. Evaluate Amazon CloudWatch metrics for CPU and memory usage. It can help you identify potential bottlenecks and manage your resources better.

2. Optimize your tasks and services. The number of CPU units used by a task and the configuration of your services influence how your resources are utilized.

3. Check and manage resource-intensive applications. Sometimes, debugging third-party applications can help in reducing CPU and

memory usage.

5.4. Task Networking Issues

A well connected ECS Task Execution flow demands a properly
configured network infrastructure. Let's look at some common
networking problems that one might face and their solutions.

When facing networking issues:

1. Check your Security Groups and NACL rules. These are the
   primary components that control inbound and outgoing traffic,
   hence ensure they're correctly configured.

2. Test connectivity. Use a utility like `telnet` to check your
   connection to the target endpoint.

3. Review Amazon ECS agent logs. They contain information about
   events relating to task state changes and can help identify
   networking issues.

5.5. Interpreting your Task's State

Interpreting your task's state is critical to troubleshooting. Here's a
brief on different task states and what you need to keep in mind:

1. Pending: A task in the `PENDING` state is preparing to enter the
   `RUNNING` state.

2. Running: `RUNNING` states indicate that the task is currently active.

3. Stopped: Check the `stoppedReason` field in the task description to
   understand why your task moved to the `STOPPED` state.

Use the `describe-tasks` command to view details about a specific task
which can help direct your troubleshooting steps.

As illustrated above, ECS Task Execution troubleshooting can be a complex, layered task, but it definitely has a structure to it. By understanding these potential issues, you can devise a troubleshooting strategy that equips you to manage and optimize your cloud infrastructure effectively. The power of ECS Task should not be feared, but harnessed.

Chapter 6. Proven Solutions for Task Failure

ECS Task Execution plays a pivotal role in orchestrating and managing containers within AWS- the Amazon Web Service. It provides a robust, scalable and secure methodology for executing tasks and services. However, not every task execution runs smoothly and issues can arise, leading to task failure. This detailed report will explore the diverse and complex world of ECS Task Execution and provide proven solutions to tackle task failure.

6.1. Analyzing Logs

One of the key features of AWS ECS is its centralized logging, which allows for real-time analysis of ECS tasks. When a task fails, AWS CloudWatch can provide valuable insights into the failure. It is essential to trace the failure through the logs, either through the AWS management console or AWS CLI.

```
$ aws logs get-log-events --log-group-name my-log-group
--log-stream-name my-log-stream
```

Through logs, you can gather significant error details. Once you have the logs captured, you can troubleshoot the potential problem.

6.2. Checking Memory Allocation

Inadequate memory allocation can be a major contributor to task failure. It results in an out of memory (OOM) error. A task cannot be run on an instance if there isn't enough memory to accommodate it.

It's of essential importance to keep reviewing your task's memory requirements periodically. This will ensure you allocate enough memory for your tasks to run efficiently.

The ensuing parameters help to alter the memory allocation, which can confirm that tasks have adequate memory:

- `memory`: This parameter is for hard limits. If a task surpasses this memory, it is killed.

- `memoryReservation`: This parameter is for soft limits. If a task surpasses this memory, it is liable to be killed when the instance runs low on memory.

6.3. Assessing Network Configuration

Often tasks may fail due to incorrect network configuration, particularly if your task relies on specific ports or security groups. It's critical to confirm that your task definition and network configuration are correctly aligned.

To assess your network configuration, use the AWS Management Console:

- Navigate to the task definition page to view the details of your network mode along with the port mappings.

Consider the following aspects while assessing the network configuration:

- A common issue is port conflicts, where the same host port is being used by multiple tasks. This is not feasible in `bridge` or `host` network modes.

- If the task relies on specific security groups, it's crucial to ensure these are correctly linked in your task definition.

6.4. Checking Task Definition Permissions

Tasks use IAM roles and policies to interact with other AWS services. If these roles or policies are changed or deleted, it can lead to task failure.

Use the AWS CLI to list the IAM role policies attached to a role:

```
$ aws iam list-attached-role-policies --role-name my-role
```

This returns a list of all policies attached to the role. Ensure all necessary permissions for your task are included here.

If the IAM role for your task is correct, validate the Task Execution IAM Role in the Task Definition page.

6.5. Validating Container Dependencies

Tasks often fail if the dependent services or resources are unresponsive or non-existent. Ensuring that all the dependent tasks are running correctly before launching your task reduces this risk.

Linking between different containers in the same task can be utilized. The `links` parameter in the task definition can help establish these links.

6.6. Understanding Timeouts

Several ECS operations come with default timeouts after which they are automatically terminated. If tasks aren't completing within the given time frame, increase your timeout settings.

To increase the timeout value:

- Navigate to the service definition page.
- Adjust the `healthCheckGracePeriodSeconds` parameter.

> It specifies the period during which the Amazon ECS service scheduler should ignore unhealthy Elastic Load Balancer target health checks after a task has first started.

6.7. Upgrading the Infrastructure

Lastly, AWS is continually upgrading its infrastructure and often releases new versions of its container agent and ECS optimized AMI. If your task is still failing despite trying all solutions, upgrading your infrastructure might be the way forward. To upgrade, you can:

- Check the latest ECS-optimized Amazon Machine Image (AMI) version from the AWS ECS developer forum.
- Update your container instance with the latest versions of your relevant AMIs.

After implementing these proven solutions, task failure should be significantly reduced. Always remember, the key is to understand, manage and optimize your cloud infrastructure incrementally. Reliable and efficient ECS Task Execution is crucial in maintaining an effective cloud architecture and these steps ensure you're equipped to tackle any task failure that comes your way.

Chapter 7. A Deep Dive into Network Configuration Issues

Within the ECS Task Execution landscape, network configuration issues pose a unique set of challenges that can potentially disrupt normal operations and hinder system performance. Navigating through this topic requires a comprehensive understanding of some core network principles and operation methodologies specific to ECS.

7.1. Understanding Network Configurations

The foundation of ECS Task Execution lies in Efficient Container Service (ECS) clusters. Before delving into the problematics, let's grasp the basics of network configurations. An ECS task networking is built upon Docker networking, and the task's network mode determines the kind of Docker network it utilizes.

Here are the different types of networks at disposal:

- **Bridge mode**: The task utilizes Docker's built-in virtual network which bridges the containers within the task with the EC2 instance.

- **Host mode**: In this mode, the task bypasses the Docker's built-in virtual network and maps container ports directly to EC2 instance's network interface.

- **Awsvpc mode**: The task gets its elastic network interface with a private IPv4 address, providing more control over network settings.

- **None mode**: The task does not get an external network interface, mainly used when tasks need to be completely isolated.

Having understood this, let's explore common network configuration challenges and their corresponding resolution strategies.

7.2. Network Mode Selection

Selecting the correct network mode is crucial. Depending on the task's need for isolation, security, and exposure, a suitable mode must be chosen. The wrong selection can lead to network communication issues.

For example, using the bridge or host mode, you'll share the network stack of the EC2 instance, which might result in traffic flow bottlenecks or compromised security. If the task requires high network isolation and security standards, the awsvpc mode would be more appropriate.

7.3. Task Placement Issues

Task placement constraints and strategies play a vital role in the network. Understanding and correctly applying these can help avoid common network configuration issues.

If tasks fail due to ENI exhaustion when using awsvpc mode, revise your task placement strategy. Place tasks on instances that have sufficient ENIs. A `distinctInstance` strategy can help ensure that tasks do not exhaust the ENIs of a single instance.

7.4. Task Scaling and Subnet Selection

Subnet selection is significant when scaling tasks. If tasks are scheduled without enough available IP addresses in a subnet or the subnet cannot support more ENIs, scaling operations will fail, hindering efficiency.

To remedy, either choose larger subnets, create more subnets, or place tasks in multiple subnets. Monitoring the number of available IPs and ENIs in each subnet can help predict and prevent scaling failures.

7.5. Firewall and Security Groups

Firewall configuration of the instances and security groups attached to the tasks perform a pivotal role. Erroneous rules can lead to communication blockages between the service and the tasks, resulting in downtime. Check for any inbound or outbound rules that could be blocking the desired traffic and adjust them as necessary.

7.6. DNS Issues

DNS resolution issues can cause tasks to be unable to communicate with external services. These can happen due to misconfiguration in the ECS service definition or Docker daemon.

When tasks are unable to resolve hostnames, ensure that DNS resolution settings are enabled in the service definition when using awsvpc mode. If tasks do not have outbound internet access, consider using Amazon's provided DNS service, or create your DNS service within VPC.

7.7. Load Balancer Configuration

If your ECS tasks are serviced by a load balancer, misconfigurations can lead to issues as well. Tasks might become unavailable if incoming traffic is not correctly routed, or health checks fail due to incorrect response expectations.

Ensure that your load balancer's listeners and target groups are correctly configured. In case of health check failures, confirm if your tasks are returning the expected response codes and have a proper grace period configured.

In conclusion, understanding the nuances of network configurations, coupled with proactive measures, can mitigate the downtime caused by common network configuration issues. As each scenario differs, consider the context of your application and your organizational needs while implementing any of these solutions.

Chapter 8. Mastering Resource Limit Challenges

Let's begin with an essential premise. Both virtual and traditional infrastructures require consistent monitoring and management of resources, essential for the optimal performance and scalability of applications. More so, understanding the way ECS tasks utilize resources such as CPU and memory can pave the way to efficient task execution.

8.1. Insights into ECS Resource Models

It's crucial to be aware that, in ECS, task-level resources are operating system-level constructs. This means that, as a task runs on an EC2 instance, it utilizes system-level resources, not those of the individual container.

Two resource models are available in ECS: task-level and container-level. Task-level resources are the most commonly used, enabling you to specify parameters at the task definition level. For instance, for a task using 512 CPU units and 2 GB of memory, it's possible to run two tasks on an EC2 instance with 1024 CPU units and 4 GB of memory, irrespective of your containers' configuration.

Container-level resources, conversely, allow you to specify resources individually for each container within a task.

Understanding these two ECS resource models, particularly the task-level version, is the first step in mastering resource limit challenges.

8.2. Overcoming Task Scheduling Failure

One common issue experienced by users is task scheduling failure due to insufficient CPU units or memory. This often happens when the resources specified in the task definition exceed what's available on the instance. The ECS scheduler cannot place the task, and an error message is generated.

The solution is twofold: either reduce the resources specified in the task definition or use an instance with more resources. Proper planner tools could also prove beneficial, as they'll provide you with insights to determine what is required for your application or service needs, thereby preventing over-provisioning.

8.3. Understanding Memory Boundaries

Amazon ECS recommends that the memory limit parameter be set for each container, with the general rule being a maximum of 10 percent greater than the hard limit for the task overall. Remember that exceeding the stated memory limit will result in the Docker daemon killing the container.

If a significant amount of your tasks are being terminated due to 'out of memory' issues, consider raising your task level memory limit. Alternatively, adjusting your application's memory consumption might be a necessary action for more efficient task execution.

8.4. Maximizing Performance with CPU Over-Provisioning

Despite conventional wisdom that suggests maximizing resource use for efficiency, it can be a strategic move to intentionally under-utilize resources, such as configuring tasks to use fewer CPU units. This strategy, called CPU over-provisioning, can significantly improveperformance by minimizing context switching—enhancing system throughput, reducing latency, and maintaining more predictable performance overall.

Bear in mind, though, that this approach may not support all use cases and might not be adequate under heavy CPU-utilization.

8.5. Mastering Fargate Resource Allocation

Successfully using Fargate involves an understanding of resource allocation. With Fargate, there are no EC2 instances to manage; resources are automatically scaled, patched, and administered, minimizing overhead while increasing security.

However, there can be challenges if your service requires high CPU utilization for extended periods. The 'Burst' mode – the Fargate capability to burst a task's CPU for a short timeframe – might not be sufficient, especially when dealing with CPU-demanding tasks.

Therefore, it's a good idea to set your Fargate tasks' CPU value above the minimum necessary requirements for optimal performance, while maintaining a good balance with cost optimization goals.

In conclusion, mastering ECS Resource Limit Challenges is fundamentally about finding a balance between available resources, cost, and application requirements. Regularly monitoring your task performance, coupled with a thorough understanding of your specific application needs, is key to effectively managing ECS task execution. If you can achieve this, you'll be well-placed to maximize the potential of your cloud infrastructure.

Chapter 9. Solving Task Scheduling Troubles

The ability to successfully schedule tasks is an integral part of using Amazon ECS. It enables you to run tasks according to your specific business needs, with the process ranging from a single task execution to thousands of tasks running concurrently. Despite its significance, task scheduling can often present troubles that might encumber smooth operations. This trouble arises due to various factors like resource constraints, configuration ambiguities, or misconceived task definitions.

9.1. Understanding Task Scheduling

Before you diagnose any scheduling troubles, it's beneficial to first comprehend the basics of task scheduling and its operational mechanisms. Task scheduling in ECS is essentially the method of distributing tasks over available resources. ECS provides you with multiple ways to schedule tasks:

1. `RunTask` operation: It can be used when you want to manually run tasks.

2. `StartTask` operation: You may use it to place tasks on specific container instances.

3. Service scheduler: Useful when you want to maintain a specified number of tasks running in a service at any given time.

To ensure the successful scheduling of tasks, ECS typically goes through several stages which include:

1. Making a scheduling decision by considering the task's CPU and memory requirements, then identifying which instances can meet these needs.

2. Finding a fitting instance for the task. If ECS can't locate one, it returns a 'RESOURCE:RESOURCE: CPU | MEMORY' error.

Intuitive understanding of these operations and stages makes diagnosing and troubleshooting scheduling-related problems easier.

9.2. Configuration Issues

Your task scheduling might fail due to some misconfigurations. A deeper look into some of these common problems can help manage them effectively.

1. `Service failing to launch tasks`: If this occurs, check your service events tab. A 'RESOURCE:RESOURCE: CPU | MEMORY' event signifies that your task's CPU and memory reservations might be too high for your instances. You can either lower the reservations or use larger instances.

9.3. Cluster Resource Limitations

If your task scheduling repeatedly fails, you may be facing resource limitations. Your cluster needs sufficient resources to function optimally and scheduling tasks beyond these available resources could lead to failure.

You can use the `DescribeClusters` API to review available resources. If the available resources are less than the task requirements, then tasks won't run. Two strategies can help resolve this:

1. `Resource augmentation`: This involves adding more resources by either creating new instances or modifying existing ones to increase memory or CPU.

2. `Task requirements reduction`: Adjust the task definition to reduce your resource requirements. Carefully review your soft and hard memory limits before adjusting.

Remember, your tasks also need the `ENI` and `IP` limits for running. Each instance has a maximum ENI and IP limit, and running out of either could halt task scheduling. Increase the limits or modify your task definition to lower the ENI/IP utilization.

9.4. Task Placement Strategies and Constraints

If the aforementioned reasons don't apply, reconsider your task placement strategies and constraints since they dictate how tasks are placed within a cluster.

1. `Task placement strategies`: Different strategies are available for task placement, like binpack, random, or spread. If tasks can't start, review your service or RunTask API task placement strategy. Changing the strategy can sometimes resolve issues.

2. `Task placement constraints`: If improperly configured, constraints can prevent task start. Check your constraint definitions carefully for any possible conflicts or infractions.

9.5. Decoding Error Messages

Sometimes, understanding the error messages can help diagnose the issue. Common error messages include:

1. `RESOURCE:RESOURCE: CPU | MEMORY`: As discussed earlier, this reveals insufficient CPU or memory resources.

2. `RESOURCE:RESOURCE: ENI`: This message signifies that you've maxed out your ENI limit.

3. `Failed to start some tasks: TASK_DEFINITION_NOT_FOUND`: This indicates a problem with your task definition.

These error messages often lead you to the root cause of the problem that you can address directly to mitigate task scheduling troubles.

By understanding the fundamentals, recognizing common issues, and learning to interpret your error messages, you can ensure efficient task scheduling, drastically improving the operations within your cloud infrastructure. Although it might seem demanding initially, deciphering your ECS environment is key to recouping full benefits from your cloud environment. The hurdles are surmountable – no trap is inescapable.

Chapter 10. Understanding Task Execution IAM Role Hurdles

The Elastic Container Service (ECS) Task Execution Identity and Access Management (IAM) roles represent one of the most frequently encountered and critical obstacles in the world of cloud infrastructure. How are they so important?

Rapid advances in cloud technologies have reshaped our perception of system architecture and data storage strategies. However, with the advent of these technologically forward strategies comes a parallel expansion of complexity. A core component of Amazon's ECS, the IAM role provides important access control middles, instrumental in proper task execution. A lucid grasp of IAM roles and policies can enable optimized task execution and, consequently, improve your cloud infrastructure's overall performance. Offering a robust solution to critical security and authorization needs, comprehending IAM roles is compelling.

10.1. Understanding IAM Roles in ECS

Before diving into the hurdles associated with IAM roles, it's imperative to understand what IAM roles are and how they function within the ECS environment. IAM stands for Identity and Access Management, a service provided by AWS for managing access to AWS services and resources. The service functions on two core ideas: IAM roles and policies.

IAM roles act as bearers of permissions, allowing services or users to adopt these roles to access specific resources. Unlike user credentials, which are associated with a single user, IAM roles can be assumed by any service that requires it.

IAM Policies attached to roles provide permissions to make API requests to AWS services. Policies themselves are documents describing specific actions allowed or denied under various conditions.

Task Execution IAM Role is a specific IAM role that grants ECS services or tasks permissions to make API calls to other necessary AWS services.

10.2. IAM Role Hurdles in Task Execution

While IAM roles offer a seamless way to manage access and ensure security, they're not without their set of challenges. From permission issues to misunderstanding roles and policies, let's explore the typical roadblocks administrators face with IAM roles in ECS task execution.

1. Inadequate or Incorrect Permissions:

Perhaps the most common hurdle, IAM roles fail to perform effectively due to insufficient permissions. Often, debugging these issues can cause significant downtime. To evade this, administrators must devote attention to detail, ensuring that the IAM roles have been assigned the correct and adequate permissions for all necessary operations.

1. Interaction with Other AWS services:

An ECS task often interacts with a variety of other AWS services (like ECR, CloudWatch, etc.). An improper service-to-service interaction often leads to execution failures. This requires task execution roles to carry the appropriate permissions associated with all the interacting services.

1. Misconfiguration of Policies:

Another common challenge is when policies attached to roles are wrongly configured, either granting increased access or completely rejecting necessary requests. Policies are equally critical as IAM roles - incorrect configuration can lead to denied access and result in unexpected failures.

10.3. Dealing with IAM Role Hurdles

Surviving the challenges thrown by IAM roles in ECS task execution requires a thorough understanding of the associated concepts and advanced troubleshooting skills. Here are some proven practices that can help you overcome IAM Role hurdles:

1. Regularly Review Permissions and Policies:

With IAM roles intricately linked to security, regular examination of permissions and policies is essential. This will help nip any potential problem in the bud and ensure the smooth functioning of your cloud infrastructure.

1. Log Examination:

Make it a habit to regularly explore CloudWatch logs, which will help you spot any IAM-related errors. Consistent logging can help identify the root cause of a failure, leading to quicker troubleshooting.

1. Leverage AWS Documentation:

Amazon's extensive documentation and guidelines can be an incredible resource. Stay updated with these instructions and adapt them to fit your cloud environment.

10.4. Learning from Real-world Scenarios

Sometimes, understanding hurdles and their solutions with examples derived from real situations can be incredibly rewarding. Let's look at a few:

Example 1: A common scenario involves ECS tasks failing to download images from ECR due to insufficient permissions. In such cases, examine if the IAM role associated with the task has the necessary `ecr:GetDownloadUrlForLayer` API permission.

Example 2: Consider ECS tasks frequently timing out. On investigation, you may find that the root cause lies in CloudWatch not having adequate permissions to write logs, because the IAM Task Execution Role doesn't have the `logs:CreateLogStream` and `logs:PutLogEvents` permissions.

Addressing IAM role challenges requires patience, precision, and deep understanding. As daunting and irritating as they may seem, these hurdles are ultimately stepping stones – guiding you to build a stable, secure, and efficient cloud environment. They are an opportunity to better understand and streamline task execution –your key to optimizing ECS and with it, your AWS cloud infrastructure. Therefore, getting a hold over IAM Role hurdles is well worth the effort.

Chapter 11. Future-Proofing Your ECS Task Execution

As we navigate through the ever-evolving landscape of cloud-computing infrastructure, it's paramount to understand the need for future-proofing your service usage. This is especially true when it comes to ECS Task Execution, given Amazon ECS's potential to serve as the backbone of your operations. Future-proofing ensures that your systems remain robust, adaptable, and appropriate for your needs as those needs grow and change.

11.1. Debunking The Future-Proof Concept

Before delving into practical steps, it's essential to debunk the misconception around future-proofing. It's not about predicting every potential scenario and accommodating for it preemptively. That, by default, is implausible. Instead, future-proofing pertains to designing your systems in a way where accommodating changes becomes less time-consuming, delicate, and costly. This involves building a flexible design, focusing on avoiding vendor lock-in, keeping an eye on emerging trends and technologies, and ensuring that your system remains adaptable.

11.2. Building a Flexible Design

A flexible design is at the heart of future-proofing. Operating in the cloud, it's vital to note that workloads can fluctuate greatly, and the ability to scale appropriately is a key feature of your system's robustness.

Amazon Elastic Container Service (ECS) offers two launch types: EC2 and Fargate. EC2 allows for user control over the underlying infrastructure while Fargate abstracts this away, managing the task execution itself. You can select the launch type per task, offering you the flexibility to fit the task to best suit your needs. This flexibility is a cornerstone component to a future-proof design, and it's vital to invest time in understanding the different task options and how they fit into your application and resource management strategy.

11.3. Avoiding Vendor Lock-in

Undoubtedly, Amazon ECS offers a robust and dependable task execution service, making it a go-to choice for a large number of organizations. Yet, one must bear in mind the inherent risk of vendor lock-in. Vendor lock-in ties you to a specific provider's tools and services, limiting your ability to switch vendors without significant operational disruption and costs.

While ECS is Amazon-specific, containerization itself is standardized. By ensuring your tasks and service definitions remain in line with these standards, you can significantly reduce the disruption if a switch becomes necessary. This standardization aids in creating a vendor-agnostic approach, a key to future-proofing your task execution.

11.4. Embrace Continuous Learning

As with any technology, optimism is encouraged, but so is skepticism. Keep an eye on emerging trends and technologies. A healthy degree of wariness about new technologies is reasonable because not all will stand the test of time. Conversely, some will, and early adopters stand to gain. Participating in technology-oriented communities, attending tech conferences, and undergoing continuous training ensures that your team stays adaptable and is well-prepared for changes.

11.5. Building for Adaptability

A future-proof ECS task execution strategy must also emphasize adaptability. When designing services and implementing tasks, your design should aim to ensure replaceability. This involves modularizing your application, following microservice best practices, and adhering to the principle of least privilege.

A future-proof ECS strategy also includes optimizing costs so they scale with your business. This could mean using Spot Instances or Savings Plans and taking full advantage of the cost-optimizing strategies Amazon ECS provides, like using auto-scaling.

11.6. Conclusion

In conclusion, future-proofing your ECS task execution isn't about constructing an unchanging, invincible system. Instead, it's about building a system that accommodates change gracefully. It leverages the best practices in design, maintainability, modularity, flexibility, continuous learning, and vendor-agnosticism to ensure that as your business grows and technology evolves, your system remains robust and adaptable.

The future of cloud services is arguably more exciting and challenging than ever, with continual advancements and shifts in the landscape. Future-proofing ECS Task Execution is no longer a nice-to-have; it's a business necessity. And with the considerations laid out in this guide, you are better equipped to face an unpredictable future head-on, ready to adapt and thrive.